Dêmis Carlos Fonseca Gomes
Valter Zotto de Andrade

Methods and resources for distance learning: using AVA Chamilo

Dêmis Carlos Fonseca Gomes
Valter Zotto de Andrade

Methods and resources for distance learning: using AVA Chamilo

ScienciaScripts

Imprint

Any brand names and product names mentioned in this book are subject to trademark, brand or patent protection and are trademarks or registered trademarks of their respective holders. The use of brand names, product names, common names, trade names, product descriptions etc. even without a particular marking in this work is in no way to be construed to mean that such names may be regarded as unrestricted in respect of trademark and brand protection legislation and could thus be used by anyone.

Cover image: www.ingimage.com

This book is a translation from the original published under ISBN 978-613-9-60398-5.

Publisher:
Sciencia Scripts
is a trademark of
Dodo Books Indian Ocean Ltd. and OmniScriptum S.R.L publishing group

120 High Road, East Finchley, London, N2 9ED, United Kingdom
Str. Armeneasca 28/1, office 1, Chisinau MD-2012, Republic of Moldova, Europe
Printed at: see last page
ISBN: 978-620-7-27880-0

DEDICATORY

I dedicate this work to my mother Irenice, for her help in all areas of my life, both professional and academic, to my father Antônio Carlos, to Professor MsC Kênya Maria, for everything she has done for me as a human being and as a professional, and to Professor Dr Damião Rocha for his guidance and dedication to his students.

ACKNOWLEDGEMENTS

I would like to thank God for giving me life, my supervisor, Prof. Valter, for his constânt and important contributions to the success of this work, my parents Antônio Carlos Gomes Rodrigues and Irenice Fonseca Gomes, and especially my mother, who spared no effort to ensure that I succeeded in my specialisation work;

To the face-to-face tutor Alessandra Escobar from EADCON, who spared no effort to help the class get to the end of this work.

To the others, friends and family, who have contributed so much to my journey as a researcher.

EPIGRAPH

3

Knowing is the task of subjects, not objects.
And it is as a subject, and only as a subject, that
man can truly know.

Paulo Freire

SUMMARY

SUMMARY

With the constant advance of technology and the emergence of distance learning in the second half of the 20th century, several areas of our society have changed: culture, health and especially education. Studying at home using teaching materials received by post was an educational revolution, bringing knowledge to the most remote populations in our country. This new constant need for the democratisation of knowledge and continuing training, associated with the use of information and communication technologies (ICTs), is making it possible to significantly expand access to education [SENASP/MJ, 2008]. However, in order for distance learning to be more meaningful, it is necessary to have well-designed materials, because they are the main interaction between the course centre (tutor, teacher) and the student, regardless of the form in which they appear: video, CD, text, internet, etc. In view of this, the purpose of this work is to create conditions in which education professionals can create materials for distance learning courses using Chamilo, a virtual learning environment (VLE) that makes it easier for distance learning professionals to manage teaching materials and publish them on the World Wide Web.

Keywords: Distance Education; Information and Communication Technology; Teaching Materials; Chamilo; Internet.

INTRODUCTION

Distance education is a type of teaching where the student and teacher are physically separated, thus requiring an interactive tool to link these actors (student/teacher). To this end, in addition to a tool (system), we need it to be interactive, adaptive (customised according to need) and, on the teaching side, to provide methods and resources for producing and preparing content (teaching material) that can provide students with courses of outstanding quality and serve as a benchmark for this type of teaching.

This research presents the AVA Chamilo, a system with high interactivity that helps its user administrators produce good quality teaching materials, reducing dropout and increasing motivation for the distance learning method.

With regard to the general objective, this work focused on the fact that the current VLEs have few interactional resources, which do not satisfactorily subsidise the courses made available in them, with poor quality teaching materials (due to the lack of system resources) and virtual environments that are very difficult for students to use.

As for the methodology, two types of research were chosen. Bibliographical research, using books, dictionaries, specialised magazines and websites. At the same time, the installation and demonstration of the use of AVA Chamilo for the production of content (teaching material) was carried out through direct observations, which we refer to here as a laboratory.

Methodologically, the method chosen was the hypothetical deductive method, i.e. proof was sought by means of a deduction from a proposed hypothesis.

As a means of organisation, this work has been divided into items and sub-items, according to the theme under analysis. Thus, the content of this work is laid out in seven items, the first being the introduction; the second, mapping paths; the third, the theoretical foundation; the fourth, the methodology used in the research; the fifth item (chapter 4) was dedicated to distance education; the sixth, was dedicated to the concept of virtual learning environment; the seventh (chapter 6) was directed to the study of Chamilo as a tool for the elaboration and production of didactic material.

CHAPTER 1

CHAMILO, WHY USE IT?

According to CENSO EAD.BR [2010], "distance learning is highly rated by former students, but drop-outs happen early, and 90 per cent of those who drop out do so before halfway through the course. Research suggests that the main reason for this is the dispute with the clock, which is more serious than the lack of money."

According to CENSO EAD.BR [2010]:

> The highly inclusive characteristics of distance education (DE), its ability to accommodate, in a mobile and modular way, the personal and professional demands of those who need to study, still face a major adversary: students' lack of time, or their difficulty in organising this time. This variable is largely responsible for school drop-outs, according to the drop-out students themselves interviewed by CENSO EAD.BR [2010].

According to data from the aforementioned survey, lack of time is still a major obstacle for those wishing to complete a distance learning course, however, SOUZA [2009] says that:

> In distance learning, the methodology is based on technology that totally or partially replaces the presence of teacher and student in the classroom. For example, the method of traditional distance learning courses is based mainly on written teaching material transmitted via the postal service. Whereas online distance learning is more dynamic, allows greater control over the process and enables interaction.

And it is in this context that this research is based, combining the best of traditional distance learning - written teaching material - with the best of online distance learning, with its dynamic nature.

Therefore, the main focus of this work is the production of teaching material through the study (use case) of the web tool (virtual learning environment) Chamilo, also showing the possibility of greater interaction between the participants (teacher/student), as well as extensive control over the teaching-learning process in an easy, fast and dynamic way, both for the administrators (teacher, tutor, etc.) and for the learners (students), with the aim of providing the latter with high-quality learning.

ParaLUCENA [2003]:

> The pages created on the Internet must have a different, more interactive logic, where everyone can interact with everyone else. It is essential that each individual, in addition to accessing

> information, make their productions available. It is necessary to encourage students to be authors and co-authors of the productions posted on the web, and not just let them play the role of passive recipients.

And it is with the same intention as Lucena that Chamilo tries to reproduce in his environment: the same experience and practicality in the classroom, with the participation of all those involved in the teaching/learning process.

CHAPTER 2

METHODOLOGY

This research is classified as qualitative, with a theoretical approach based on a bibliographical review with a direct approach that will cover the nature of the best use of VLEs for the production of teaching material for Distance Education, and also a case study, of a practical nature with field research (laboratory).

As for the methodology, the hypothetical-deductive method was adopted for this research. This methodology was chosen in view of the fact that proof is sought through deduction where a hypothesis has been proposed, i.e. the use of VLEs for the production and publication of teaching material aimed at better quality courses in distance learning.

As a procedure, this work was carried out through direct observations, through documentary research in books, websites, laws, ordinances, dictionaries, among others, and also through laboratory research, with the installation and use on a remote server (on the web) of the Chamilo platform, the VLE that is the subject of this research's use case.

The phases that guided this study were:

1. Identification of the research problem involving the development of better quality teaching materials for distance learning;

2. Diagnostics and data collection (bibliographical);

3. Analysing the data obtained;

4. Installation and use of the AVA Chamilo, the tool that is the object of the use case;

5. Presentation of the advantages of preparing teaching material using the Chamilo VLE to produce courses of excellence in distance learning.

CHAPTER 3

DISTANCE LEARNING

3.1 CONCEPTS

There is a lot of discussion about issues related to distance learning, and educators need to rethink the concept of this type of teaching.

According to ALVES; LAGO; NOVA [2003], distance learning is any form of construction and/or transmission of knowledge without the simultaneous presence of those involved (teacher-student) in that action. However, with the institutionalisation of formal teaching (face-to-face, with a pre-defined time and place), this concept has evolved into an even more complex form. Still according to ALVES; LAGO; NOVA [2003], distance learning would now refer only to those teaching modalities in which the teaching/learning process is no longer linked to the physical presence of students in educational institutions, catering for an audience that, for various reasons, does not have the possibility of attending these establishments at a predefined time and place.

Distance learning then emerged and was realised through multiple media, whether radio, TV, mail, telephone, internet, among others.

According to BRITO [2003], the success of distance learning courses does not depend solely on the technology used, because many educational experiences for distance learning do not achieve the expected success due to various factors unrelated to the technological means used. However, it cannot be denied that the emergence of new information and communication technologies has significantly contributed to the growth and popularisation of distance learning.

3.2 A BRIEF HISTORY

As already mentioned, distance learning arose from the need to cover a segment of the population not adequately served by the traditional education system.

Historically, according to NUNES [2009] and FREITAS [2005], the first recorded introduction of this new method of distance learning were shorthand classes[1] by correspondence, given by Calleb Philips in 1728 in the United States, who sent his lessons weekly to enrolled students. According to NUNES [2009], in 1840, Isaac Pitman also offered a shorthand correspondence course in Great Britain, and in 1880 Colege offered a preparatory course for public examinations by correspondence, which was then also offered in Russia and by various American universities such as Wisconsi, Oregon, Kansas, as well as the renowned Oxford and Cambridge in Great Britain. University extension and technical courses were the most successful.

In Brazil, according to FREITAS [2005], the Instituto Universal Brasileiro, which began its activities in 1940, seems to be the oldest institution running correspondence courses. Since then, other institutions of this kind have been created, such as the Padre Reus Institute founded in 1974 and the Centre for Regular Studies in 1981.

However, the major impetus for the evolution of distance-learning came in the mid-1960s, with the institutionalisation of secondary and higher education, starting in France and England and spreading to other countries. In Brazil, in the 1960s, this expansion took place when the Brazilian Communications Code was enacted in 1967, through Decree Law[0] 236/97, and in 1970 through the Education Guidelines and Bases Law (LDB),[0] 5.692/71, making it possible for supplementary education to be provided through the use of technologies such as radio, TV and the already conceptualised correspondence, as well as other means of communication.

In today's distance learning, the trend is to combine various media (internet, TV, audio, etc.) and use them in a single course or programme, but printed

---

[1] Tachygraphy - according to the Houaiss dictionary, it is a form of writing words using signs that allow for quick notes.

text and written communication are still basic requirements, they give students a lot of confidence in this type of teaching and cannot be underestimated.

13

CHAPTER 4

VIRTUAL LEARNING ENVIRONMENT (VLA)

4.1 - CONCEPTS

Virtual learning environment (VLE) is currently a term widely used by educators, communicators and information and communication technology professionals linked to education.

> Virtual Learning Environments (VLEs) are internet-based educational *software* designed to support distance learning activities. This *software* offers a set of information and communication technologies that allow activities to be developed at the time, space and pace of each participant. [OLIVEIRA, 2009].

According to the Aurélio dictionary of the Portuguese language, we can understand environment as everything that is around us, the environment in which we live. Virtual, according to Aurélio, comes from the Latin *virtualis* and means that which has not been realised but is susceptible of being realised, derived in turn from *virtus,* which means power, strength.

According to SANTOS [2009], "A virtual environment is a fertile space of meaning where human beings and technical objects interact, thus enhancing the construction of knowledge, and therefore learning".

With the rapid development of ICT, various virtual environments have been created: learning communities, forums, teaching portals, discussion lists, cities of knowledge and many others. And so, as is the main objective of this work, we are always looking to develop new educational methodologies, and according to OKADA [2002], "which favour the cognitive and social development of individuals, with a view to the collective and collaborative construction of knowledge. To do this, it is necessary to promote new strategies for selecting what is relevant, exchanging experiences, discussing, critically reflecting on information that is shared, processed and distributed, in real time or not, as well as articulating different meanings and senses, deconstructing and reconstructing new knowledge".

What about cyberspace, how does it relate to VLEs?

> Digitised information is reproduced, circulated, modified and updated at different interfaces. It is possible to digitise sounds, images, graphics, texts, in short, an infinite amount of information. [SANTOS, 2002].

It is in this context that we find cyberspace. It represents the medium through which information flows digitally. And it is through the world wide web that we find its main function: interconnection.

> Cyberspace is much more than a means of communication or media. It brings together, integrates and resizes a multitude of media and interfaces. We can find media such as: newspapers, magazines, radio, cinema and TV, as well as a plurality of interfaces that allow synchronous and asynchronous communications, such as chats, lists and discussion forums, blogs, among others. In this sense, as well as being structured as a universal virtual learning environment that connects socio-technical networks around the world, cyberspace allows groups/subjects to form virtual communities founded for very specific purposes, such as online learning communities. [SANTOS, 2002].

Throughout the growing distance education market in Brazil and around the world, many VLEs can be found in cyberspace, i.e. on the Internet. The following table shows some well-known VLEs, with formats and costs that vary according to users' needs.

Table 01 - Examples of some VLEs available worldwide

AVA	Organisation/Author	Virtual Address
Moodle	Free software, idealised by Martin Dougiamas	www.moodle.org
Blackboard	Blackboard (USA)	www.blackboard.com
CoSE	StaffordshireUniversity (United Kingdom)	www.staffs.ac.uk/COSE/
Teleduc	Unicamp NIED (Brazil)	www. tel educ.org.br/
Chamilo	Software book	www.chamilo.org

It's important to note that we can't just analyse VLEs as technological tools, but also the attitude of the managers and authors of the learning community. You can find an incredible variety of pedagogical and communication practices on the Internet.

With their tools, VLEs enable the production of content and a variety of information and communication channels, database management, as well as total control of the information that passes through and into the environment. It is in this context that this work is based. The use of good practice for the production of quality teaching materials through the use of a VLE.

CHAPTER 5

CHAMILO

5.1 THE EVOLUTION OF LMS

According to MAES [2010], the Chamilo VLE emerged in 2010 from its predecessor, Dokeos. Dokeos is an open source LMS that receives contributions from universities, schools and other institutions, as well as individuals. It has been widely used in Europe and Latin America and is well known for having a wide range of functions, especially ease of use, speed and stability. However, many developers realised that the LMS, or AVA, created in 1999, still under the name Claroline (Classroom On-Line), had a number of drawbacks and limitations. Dokeos is based on courses, where data is limited to these courses, and there is no central content management system that stores all learning objects, including documents, images, sounds, assessments and all possible learning objects.

For these reasons, the use of Dokeos in the face of the current needs of distance education has been discussed, with growing dissatisfaction among users and developers with the tool's lack of structure and the release of only a very limited commercial version.

And so, in January 2010, the developers split up, with the majority opting to develop a new project, also open source, and Chamilo was born, a system that organises teaching and learning processes through instructional and interactional content in a collaborative way.

According to MAES[2010], Chamilo means "chameleon", one that can adapt to the environment in which it lives. Chamilo is also a non-profit organisation governed by the laws of its country of creation, Belgium. This association brings together companies, universities, schools and other educational institutions, either as a partner or as a user.

The first version of Chamilo appeared with 1.8.6.2, succeeding Dokeos 1.8.6.1, enabling Dokeos users to switch smoothly to the new system. According to MAES [2010], "the aim was to build a web-based learning system, with a collaboration platform that was easy to use and integrate, with the great advantage over its predecessor (Dokeos) being the reuse of resources".

For the Chamilo developers, there is more than a need to accommodate groups, projects and files, there is a clear need to have educational resources in electronic form to be reusable, in the broadest sense. In addition, the developers wanted the new platform to be as generic as possible, making it such a flexible tool that it could be easily adapted to different environments, both in educational institutions and in companies.

Chamilo interacts with different elements in its environment, such as the web server, database, file system and so on. Like any system, Chamilo requires actions to be taken to post, monitor its operation and maintain its components.

5.2- STARTING CHAMILO

According to the CHAMILO ADMINISTRATION GUIDE[2010], Chamilo is a web application designed on the LAMP platform:
- Linux: Operating system most commonly used as the platform's server, also with free source code;
- Apache: The most widely used web server for Unix platforms;
- MySQL: Relational, multi-user database used by the Chamilo platform;
- PHP: programming language initially developed for creating web pages with a book software licence, as shown in the figure below.

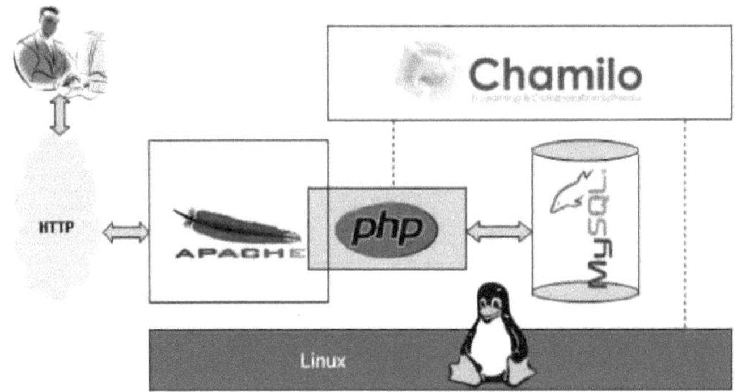

Figure 01 - Call for LAMP

As it is free software, Chamilo is designed to run on free platforms and can also be used on operating systems such as Windows and Mac (proprietary operating systems).

To demonstrate the key object of this research use case, Chamilo 1.8.8.4 was installed, using EasyPHP version 5.3.6.O. EasyPHP is a tool (development kit) that sets up a web server on the installed machine (computer), providing the developer with Apache (web server), MySQL (database server), PHPMyAdmin (database administration tool) and PHP (set of scripts used to develop web applications).

Once EasyPHP has been installed and is running, we move on to installing Chamilo, which we obtained free of charge from *http://www.chamilo.org* and installed as shown in the following figures.

Figure 02 - First Chamilo installation screen

Figure 03 - Second phase of the installation: choosing the language

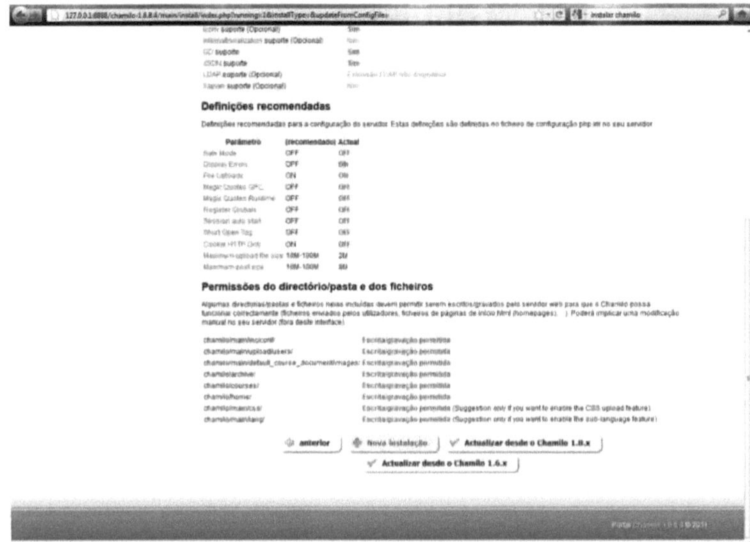

Figure 04 - Third stage: checking the minimum requirements for installation

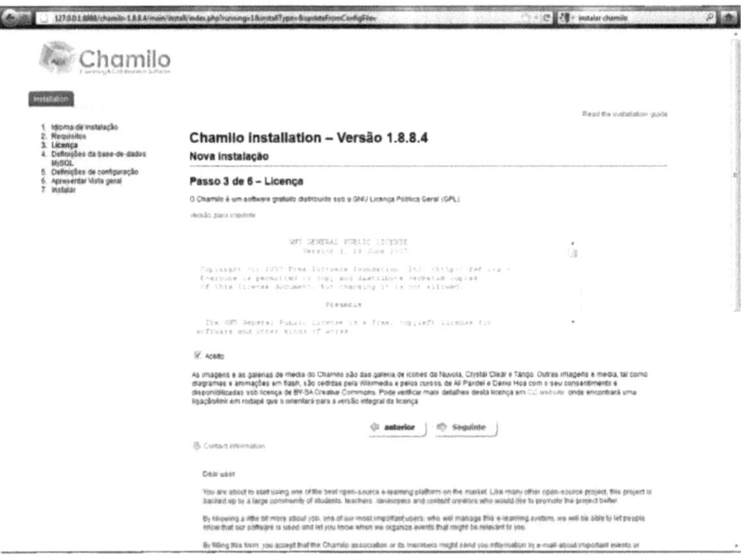

Figure 05 - Fourth phase: as this is free software distributed under the GNU licence, it is

necessary to accept its terms

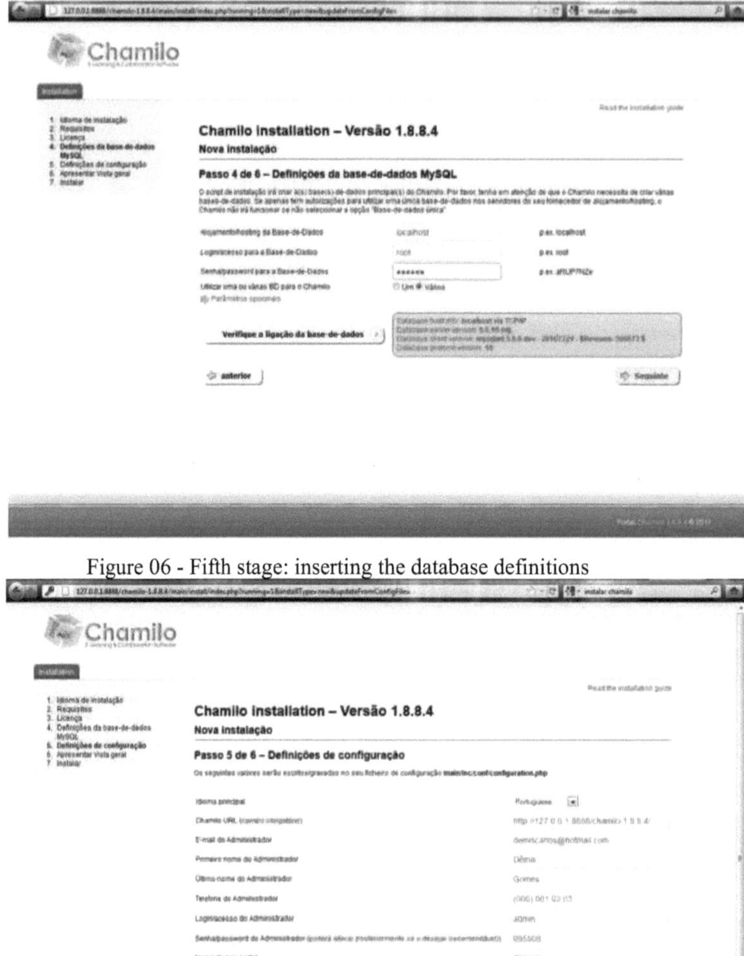

Figure 06 - Fifth stage: inserting the database definitions

Figure 07 - Sixth step: including the platform administrator's data

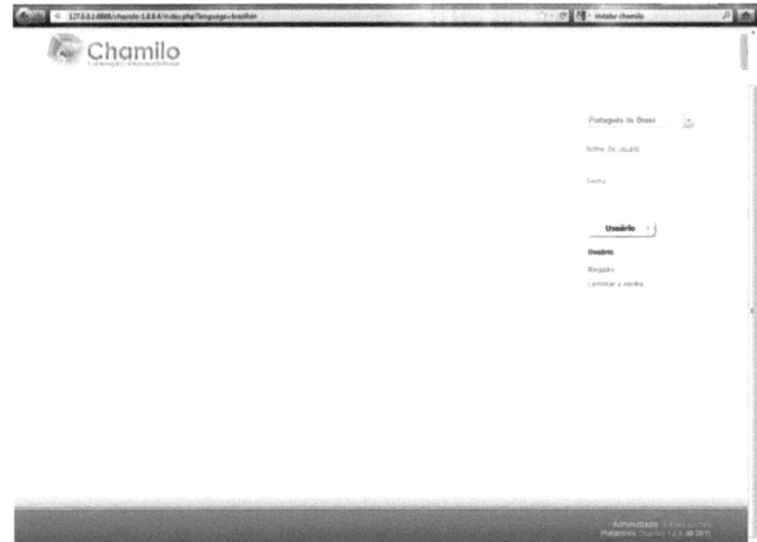

Figure 08 - Chamilo platform already installed and ready for use

5.3- 0 CHAMYL AND ITS ELEMENTS

Chamilo is a system for teaching and learning based on the use of the web, known as e-learning (virtual learning). As such, it has tools for use and others for administration.

According to the CHAMILO ADMINISTRATION GUIDE [2010], in order to better understand its management tools, we must first have a clear idea of its needs and the elements that must be managed.

According to the CHAMILO ADMINISTRATION GUIDE [2010], The fundamental elements on which Chamilo is based are users, courses and sessions.

5.3.1- USERS

In order to interact with Chamilo, the user must be registered as a user. Every user registered on the platform (AVA) has a role, and the privileges they have in the system are determined for them.

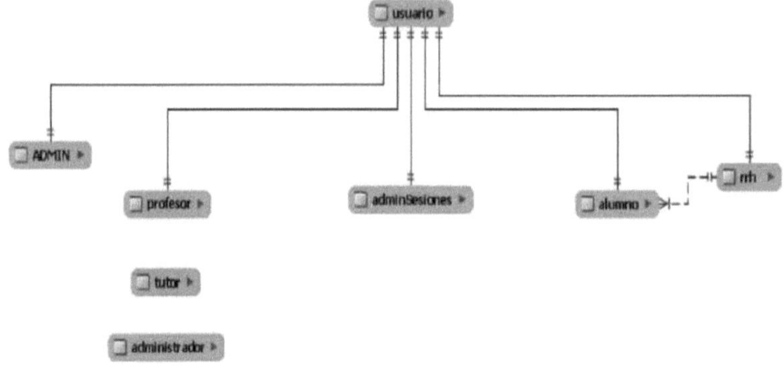

Figure 09 - Types of Chamilo users

Certain types of user can have more than one role and certain roles allow them to take on one or more different roles, with fewer privileges.

5.3.1.1- THE ADMINISTRATOR

The ADMIN user illustrated in figure 9 is the system administrator. The administrator account was created to install Chamilo and has full privileges over the system. According to the CHAMILO ADMINISTRATION GUIDE [2010], ADMIN is the highest-ranking user, and no-one can change or delete it except other system administrators.

To summarise, the ADMIN will have the following functions or tasks during their shift:

1. Understand the system administration process as a whole;
2. Create new courses;
3. Generate reports;
4. Identify and resolve interface problems;
5. Creating and registering user accounts;
6. Creating sessions;

7. Modify the space limits of the courses;

8. Check the students' results and whether they have handed in their work on time;

9. Assist the students;

10. Manage uploads of student activity files.

5.3.1.2-THE TEACHER

According to the CHAMILO ADMINISTRATION GUIDE [2010], the PROFESSOR user is the second most important in the Chamilo hierarchy, but is not the second user with the most privileges.

The TEACHER is the user with privileges to create courses within the environment. The teacher can teach their courses and carry out certain administration activities. A teacher can also at some point take on the role of system administrator, tutor and student, the latter in two contexts: within their own course, to find out what their students think of it, and if a teacher is part of another teacher's course, in which case the teacher has student privileges.

5.3.1.3   - THE SESSION MANAGER

In Chamilo, sessions are tools available for organising groups of students and associating them with a set of courses. These sessions can be time-limited and supervised by a tutor who will have access to information and interaction tools. A session can have one or more administrators, who can manage one or more sessions. Just as a session can have one or more students and a student can be enrolled in one or more sessions.

To better understand the concept of sessions in Chamilo, the CHAMILO ADMINISTRATION GUIDE [2010] mentions that there are two types of use of sessions: use for university courses and use for individual courses of fixed duration. In the case of university courses, the session is represented by a group of students following one or more courses, with the help of teachers assigned to administer these (courses), and these sessions, or cycles, are the periods of time we know today as semesters or terms. For example: the students of the 5° period of the Computer Science course at a university represent a session in Chamilo, where "50" represents the category of the session, the group of students participating in the 50 period represent the cycle, or session, and the lecturer is the tutor, or session administrator.

As for the use of sessions for individual courses of fixed duration, one session per student can be defined and a tutor assigned to this student. The session administrator is responsible for assigning

5.3.1.4   -THE TUTOR

The tutor's role in Chamilo is to teach courses that have not been created by the tutor (created by the teacher user). The tutor's privileges can be extended or reduced, according to what has been agreed with the course teacher.

5.3.1.5-STUDENT

This is the user with the lowest level of privilege in the system. They are only enrolled in the courses, i.e. they are only participants in the teaching-learning process through Chamilo.

5.3.1.6- HUMAN RESOURCES MANAGER

This user, according to the CHAMILO ADMINISTRATION GUIDE [2010], is a special user and is somewhat outside the privileges scheme mentioned above. He (rrh) has the ability to supervise the Students user segment and report the results of this supervision.

5.3.2- COURSES

The course is the basic element in organising content and interactions.

A course is created and to some extent managed by a teacher, and can be taught by that teacher or by one or more tutors, where the latter can teach one or more courses. The following figure shows the courses that the user who accessed the system is enrolled in, and you can also see the name of the teacher for each course.

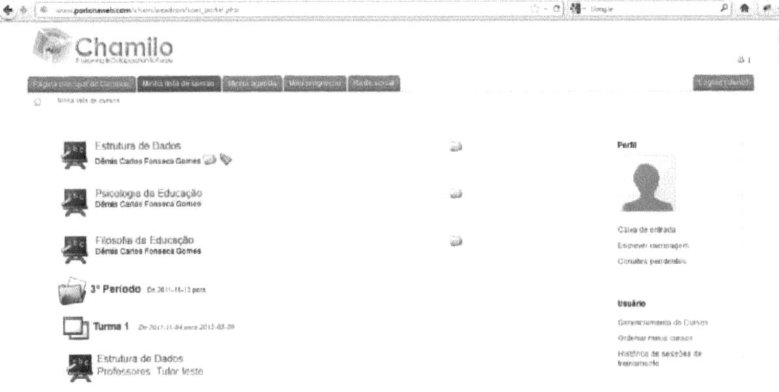

Figure 10 - Courses in which the logged-in user is enrolled

5.3.3- NAVIGATION

The navigation elements are the considerable part that makes Chamilo so easy to use. According to the CHAMILO ADMINISTRATION GUIDE [2010] this navigation is divided into four parts:

1. Main menu tabs and header links;

2. Breadcrumb;

3. Main content;

4. Footer.

The main menu tabs (header links) are (by definition and can be changed):

home page, my courses, my diary, social networks, reports and platform administration.

5.3.4- BREADCRUMB

It is a feature that shows the path of the pages visited, indicating to the student which session they are in within the system, where they will see something like: CComp Course > Documents > Books.

5.3.5 - HOME PAGE

Figure 11 shows the Chamilo home page with all its functionalities.

5.3.6 - FOOTER

The footer contains information about the system administrator as well as an indication of the version of Chamilo being used.

5.4- PUBLISHING CONTENT ON THE PLATFORM

What was called a "laboratory" was created for this session of the research. Using a domain already registered on the web (http://www.portonaweb.com), the subdomain /chamiloeadcon was created for the installation and demonstration of the VLE being researched.

Once Chamilo had been installed on the remote server (http://www.portonaweb.com/chamiloeadcon), we began to feed the system by creating courses with their content, files and relevant information.

With the system in operation, and following Chamilo's concept that only (until privileges are changed) the TEACHER user has the privilege of creating courses and administering them, the main user with the status of TEACHER was created in the VLE installation.

To start a publication, as with all platforms, the user must be registered in the system's database, where they have a login (username) and password to access the course and its contents.

Once logged in, the teacher will have access to the courses they administer.

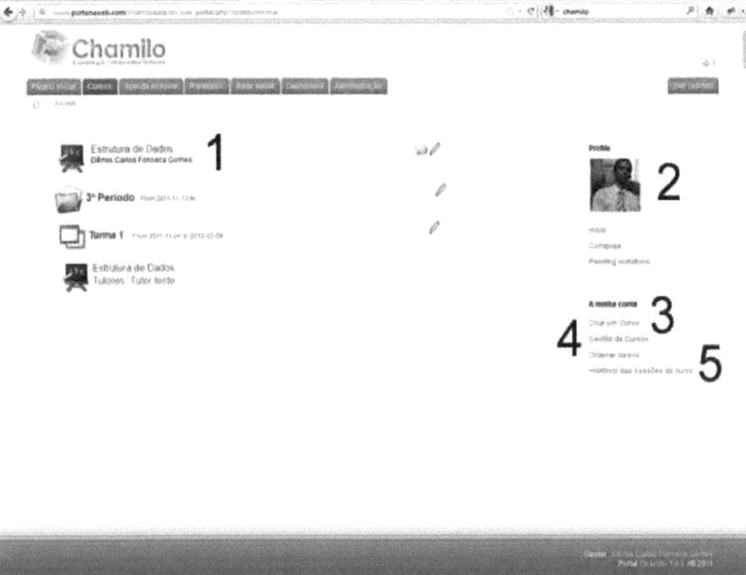

Figure 11- My courses

Figure 11 illustrates the "My Courses" tab selected after the PROFESSOR user has entered the Chamilo platform. In 1 we see the list of courses the user is on. In 2 we see links to social networks. In 3, the TEACHER has the link that allows him to create courses, in 4, the TEACHER, who can also be a student, has the possibility of enrolling in courses and in 5 we have a page dedicated to the history of course sessions.

To demonstrate the Chamilo platform, we will create a course and show how to post content, demonstrating how easy it is to advertise both from the teaching side (TEACHER) and from the student side (STUDENT).

5.4.1- CREATING A COURSE

Creating a course is simple and quick. After logging in as a TEACHER, just click on "Create a Course", fill in the required fields and the course will be visible to the creator and the users enrolled in it. It is at this point in the creation process that we select the type of teaching material used in the course, text, multimedia and so on.

According to CHAMILO 1.8.7.1 - TEACHER'S MANUAL [2010], it is very important when creating a course to limit full access to the course to viewers (students), giving them specific access privileges, such as access only to registered users, enrolment only by the course administrator and so on.

5.4.2- CONTENT CREATION

It is through the "My Courses" tab that Chamilo gives us the possibility of creating courses and managing their content. This is where we find the platform's main distance learning tools for interacting with students: course description, learning routes, exercises, assessments, calls, documents, links, announcements, glossary, diary, forums, wiki, chat, among others.

From a course created on the platform, we move on to teacher/student interactions. The figure below illustrates the access links to the tools mentioned.

Figura 12   - Chamilo's distance learning tools

Among the various tools for creating content (teaching material), the main ones can be mentioned:

- "Course description": a summary of the course in which the student is participating;
- "Learning routes": a place where the student can find all the material related to the lessons, such as text, slides, videos, audio, tests, activities and other materials used as a basis for the subject;
- "Documents": a place where you can find all the files available for download, organised by learning route, offering students the facility to have all the lesson content for a given course in a single file and study it anywhere, or even print it out;
- Forums: space for discussions between student/student, teacher/student and so on;
- Exercises and assessments: spaces where students can answer questions directly in the system, with answers at the end of each test, and with the result (grade) obtained.

For better clarification and as a demonstration of the laboratory session of this research, a course called "Data Structure" was created: with one lesson and a two-question exercise.

31

After entering the description of how the course would be taught in the "Course Description" section (syllabus, general and specific objectives, programme content, methodology, bibliography and assessment methods), we moved on to publishing the main teaching material for the course, which was made up of texts and published using the "Learning Routes" tool, as can be seen in the figure below.

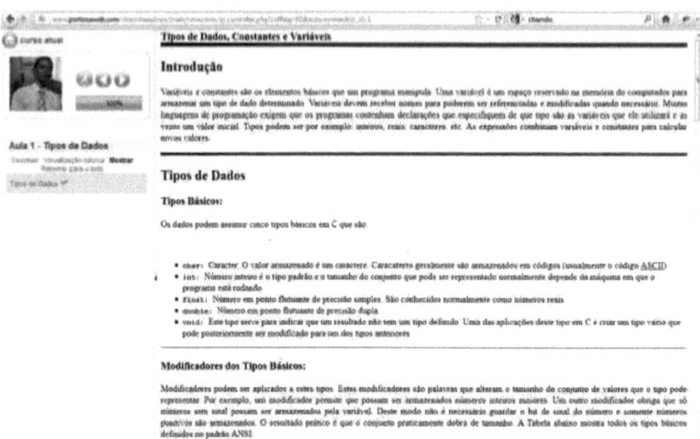

Figure 13 - Lesson 1 of the Data Structure course

The "Learning Routes" tool allows students to visualise the entire course in a very structured, simple and easy-to-understand way (in chapters). Using the "Exercises" tool, an exercise was created for this demonstration, referring to lesson 1 of the Data Structure course, with two questions, as shown in figure 14, and in figure 15 the result with the grade obtained by the student.

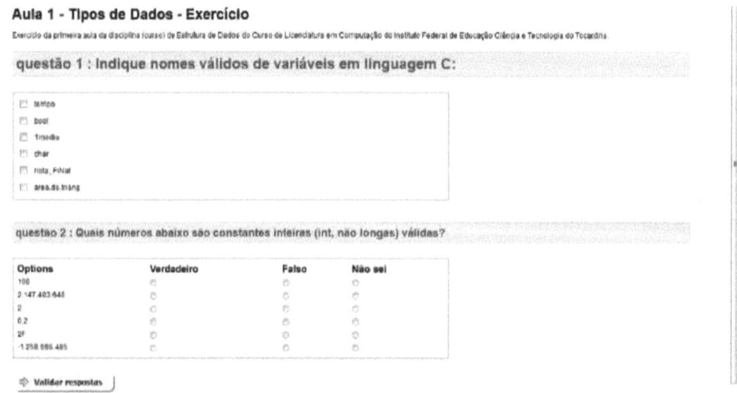

Figure 14 - Exercise from Lesson 1 of the Data Structure course with one question of the multiple answer type and another of the multiple answer type true, false or don't know

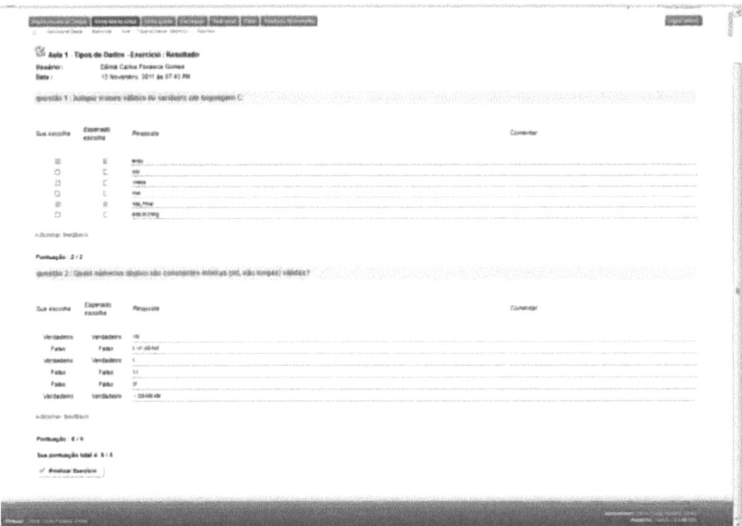

Figura 15   - Result of the exercise from Lesson 1 of the Data Structure course

As it is an *open-source* system, Chamilo gives users the power to change it, without prior authorisation, for study purposes and to contribute to the platform's growth.

CHAPTER 6

FINAL CONSIDERATIONS

Distance education in Brazil is and has been for many years one of the most effective ways of acquiring and disseminating knowledge, where cost, time and place are the main preponderant points when choosing this type of teaching.

Since the emergence of distance education, the advance of technology has contributed greatly to this type of learning becoming increasingly popular.

With the use of correspondence to send material, over the years there has been a need for more dynamic teacher/student interaction, so that the information is brought to the student and the student returns to the teacher what has been abstracted.

Then came television and the internet, bringing quality and credibility to courses that before could only be taken in person.

With the advent of the internet, the tools used today, such as *chat,* forums, *wiki*'s, discussion lists and others, are increasingly facilitating teaching methodology. However, in order to have courses with a high standard of excellence, it is necessary for all of them to be in a single environment to facilitate learning, an environment referred to during the research as the Virtual Learning Environment (VLE).

Several VLEs were mentioned in this research, but most of them are poorly based on pedagogical theories, with few resources and do not practically reproduce the same experience carried out in the classroom, with flawed teaching materials, low collaborative interaction and tools that do not encourage students to stay in the courses, causing evasion and discredit in relation to the teaching material seen and consequently to the teaching modality (distance learning).

Therefore, this study proposed the presentation of a VLE that was intuitive, self-explanatory, with greater interaction, subsidising the development of good quality teaching material to provide excellent teaching.

The Chamilo system was then shown to be an easy, free, secure system with high interactive capacity, offering teachers tools that subsidise the creation of high-quality teaching materials and students access to these materials, making learning more meaningful and rewarding.

The work was carried out through bibliographical research and practical laboratory work, where the system was installed and its main tools for content creation were demonstrated.

Since its creation in 2010, Chamilo has been used by more than 25 countries, with more than 100,000 users around the world.

And so, by carrying out this research, we believe that we can raise awareness of the Chamilo tool as a VLE with great power for the distance learning community, advertising the idea of a free system that is easy to use and that is increasingly winning over those who work with distance learning and aim to produce good teaching materials for high-quality courses.

CHAPTER 7

BIBLIOGRAPHICAL REFERENCES

NUNES, Ivônio Barros. The History of Distance Education in the World, In: LITTO, Fredric Michael; FORMIGA, Manuel Marcos Maciel. Distance Education: the state of the art. São Paulo: Pearson Education do Brasil, 2009, p.2-8.

BRAZILIAN ASSOCIATION OF TECHNICAL STANDARDS. NBR 6023: Information and Documentation - References - Elaboration. Rio de Janeiro, 2002.

BRAZILIAN ASSOCIATION OF TECHNICAL STANDARDS. NBR 10520: Information and Documentation - Quotations in Documents - Presentation. Rio de Janeiro, 2000.

BRAZILIAN ASSOCIATION OF TECHNICAL STANDARDS. NBR 14724: Information and Documentation - Academic Papers - Presentation. Rio de Janeiro, 2002.

EASY PHP. Apache, MySQL, PHP and PHPMyAdmin.   Available at: <http://www.easyphp.org>. Accessed on 25 October 2011.

SANTOS. Edméa Oliveira dos. Virtual learning environments: for free, plural authorship. RevistaFAEBA, v.12, no. 18.2003 (in press).

. Virtual learning environments: problematising curricular practices. Salvador: UNEB Publishing House, 2003.

MAES, Jean-Marie. Chamilo 2.0: A second generation open source e-learning and collaboration platform, Ghent, Belgium, University College Ghent, 2010.

CHAMILO. Chamilo: E-Learning & Collaboration Software. Available at <http://www.chamilo.org>. Accessed on 25 October 2011.

. Chamilo Administration Guide 1.8.7.1, Available at <http://www.chamilo.org>. Accessed on 28 October 2011.

MARINS, Vania. *et al.* Game design for use in distance learning. CVA Digital Magazine, volume 4, number 13, 2007.

OSWALDO CRUZ, Foundation. Preparation of printed teaching material for distance learning programmes: guidelines for authors. Fiocruz, 2005.

ABED, Brazilian Distance Education Association. Censo ead.br. São Paulo: Pearson Education do Brasil, 2010.

MACHADO, Glaucio José Couri - organiser. Education and cyberspace: studies, proposals and challenges. Aracajú: Virtus, 2007.

SENASP/MJ, National Secretariat for Public Security. Course on preparing materials for distance education. Brasília: Fábrica de Cursos, 2008.

NOVA, Cristiane; ALVES, Lyn - organisers. Education and Technology: treading paths. Salvador: Editora da UNEB, 2003.

LAGO, Andrea; NOVA, Cristiane; ALVES, Lyn. Distance education and interactive communication. Salvador: Editora da UNEB, 2003.

BRITO, Mário Sérgio da Silva. Technologies for distance learning via the Internet. Salvador: Editora da UNEB, 2003.

OKADA, Alexandra. Virtual maps: collaborative learning environments. Salvador: Editora da UNEB, 2003.

LUCENA, Simone de. The Internet as a space for building knowledge. Salvador: Editora da UNEB, 2003.

HOUAISS. Houaiss Dictionary of the Portuguese Language. Rio de Janeiro-RJ. Antônio Houaiss Institute. Ed. Objetiva, 2001.

SANTOS, Elaine Maria dos; NETO, José Dutra de Oliveira. Dropout in distance education: identifying causes and proposing prevention strategies. Paidéia: Scientific Journal of Distance Education, volume 2, number 2, 2009.

ALVES, Lyn; BARROS, Daniela; OKADA, Alexandra. Moodle: pedagogical strategies and case studies. Salvador: EDUNEB Publishing House, 2009.

POSSARI, Lúcia Helena Vendrúsculo; NEDER, Maria Lúcia Cavalli. Didactic material for distance education: production process. Cuiabá: EdUFMT, 2009.

OLIVEIRA, Renata Frozza. Designing the student experience: interface design for Virtual Learning Environments. Novo Hamburgo: Feevale University Centre, 2009.

SOUZA, Conceição Aparecida Nascimento de. Um estudo sobre as principais causas na educação a distância - EaD. (Master's dissertation in Public Administration) - Getúlio Vargas Foundation, 2009.

Printed by Books on Demand GmbH, Norderstedt / Germany